Book Study Facilitator's Guide

for

What's Your Evidence?

Engaging K–5 Students in Constructing Explanations in Science

Carla Zembal-Saul

The Pennsylvania State University

Katherine L. McNeill

Boston College

Kimber Hershberger

State College Area School District, PA

PEARSON

Boston Columbus Indianapolis New York San Francisco Upper Saddle River
Amsterdam Cape Town Dubai London Madrid Milan Munich Paris Montreal Toronto
Delhi Mexico City São Paulo Sydney Hong Kong Seoul Singapore Taipei Tokyo

4 5 6 7 8 9 10   V069   16 15 14

ISBN 10: 0-13-212059-3
ISBN 13: 978-0-13-212059-3

Contents

Introduction

The purpose of the *Book Study Facilitator's Guide* is to provide ideas on how to conduct a Book Study group or professional development series to accompany the book *What's Your Evidence? Engaging K–5 Students in Constructing Explanations in Science* by Carla Zembal-Saul, Katherine L. McNeill, and Kimber Hershberger. Current science reform documents and standards argue for the importance of students being able to generate scientific evidence, explain natural phenomena, and participate in science talk and science writing. Critical as they are, these are challenging scientific practices for students to engage in and for teachers to plan for and implement in class. Engaging in Book Study can help teachers better support their students in these key aspects of science learning.

There are two goals of this guide: (1) to support the development of a collaborative teacher community whose members share a common interest and support one another in their work; and (2) to link the ideas presented in the book to classroom practice in which students construct scientific explanations in both writing and talk. This *Book Study Facilitator's Guide* provides an avenue for colleagues to discuss the ideas in the book, try out the scientific explanation framework (i.e., claim, evidence, reasoning, and rebuttal) with their students, and bring back student work and video clips to discuss how to continue to improve their practice. The purpose of the guide is not to cover every idea discussed in the book, but rather to extend the key ideas and provide suggestions on how to discuss those ideas in a teacher community and how to try out the ideas in classrooms. The Book Study model provides an excellent opportunity for professional development in which teachers are able to consider and apply current research to their own classrooms.

Structure of the *Facilitator's Guide*

The *Facilitator's Guide* consists of nine sessions. Table 1 provides a summary of the sessions, topic foci, and related book chapters.

Most sessions align with one chapter in the book, with the exception that Sessions 2 and 3 both align with Chapter 2 and Sessions 7 and 8 both align with Chapter 6. Since Chapter 2 provides the initial introduction to the scientific explanation framework, it would be beneficial to spend two sessions supporting participants' understanding of this essential chapter if there is time. Developing an understanding of claim, evidence, reasoning, and rebuttal is important for all of the ideas in the later chapters and the activities in the later sessions. Yet if time is limited, Sessions 2 and 3 could be combined into one session. We also find that assessment can be a challenging topic, which is why we developed two sessions to go along with Chapter 6. The first session focuses on developing assessment items while the second session focuses on developing rubrics and using the rubrics to assess student work. However, if time is limited, these two sessions could also be combined into one session.

Table 1: Book Study Sessions for Supporting Scientific Explanations

Session	Topic	Related Book Chapter	
1	Importance of supporting students in scientific explanations	Chapter 1:	The Importance of Engaging K–5 Students in Scientific Explanation
2	Understanding the scientific explanation framework	Chapter 2:	A Framework for Explanation-Driven Science
3	Introducing the scientific explanation framework to students	Chapter 2:	A Framework for Explanation-Driven Science
4	Planning for explanation-driven science	Chapter 3:	Planning for Explanation-Driven Science
5	Scaffolding scientific talk and writing	Chapter 4:	Supporting Scientific Talk and Writing
6	Instructional sequence and teaching strategies	Chapter 5:	Integrating Scientific Explanation into Classroom Instruction
7	Designing scientific explanation assessments	Chapter 6:	Designing Assessment Tasks and Rubrics
8	Designing and using rubrics	Chapter 6	Designing Assessment Tasks and Rubrics
9	Supporting learning over time	Chapter 7:	Fostering a Community of Your Scientists over Time

Unlike a traditional book club in which participants gather to talk about a book they have already read, these sessions are intended to be a constructivist-oriented learning experience in which teachers read the chapters after the session. We structured each session so that participants can build their own understandings of the key ideas through conducting investigations, analyzing video, examining student work, designing learning tasks, and designing assessment tasks with their colleagues. These activities introduce the essential concepts to participants. After engaging in these experiences during the workshops, participants then read the corresponding chapter in order to reinforce, extend, and apply what they have learned to new contexts and examples. Reading the book then allows participants to develop a more in-depth understanding of how to apply the ideas to their own classrooms.

Schedule and Time

The suggested length of each session is 1.5 hours. These sessions could occur after school, during half days, on the weekends, or during shared time during the school day. The first three sessions could also occur during the summer before the school year starts. Starting with Session 3, the homework involves trying different ideas in the participants' classrooms, and bringing in samples of student writing or video. Consequently, the recommendation is that these later sessions occur during the school year. Furthermore, there should be a couple of weeks or a month between these later sessions to allow the participants time to try out the ideas in their classrooms and to collect student work, which they will bring to the next meeting to analyze as a group.

Although the suggested length includes nine sessions of 1.5 hours each (total 13.5 hours), the sessions can be adapted or combined in different ways to meet the scheduling needs of the participants. For example, if a group is able to meet only four times, it could meet the first time for 4 hours and each subsequent meeting for 3 hours. Table 2 provides a potential adapted schedule.

Another possibility is that a group is able to meet more than 8 times or 13.5 hours over the course of the summer and school year. In this case, some sessions can actually be repeated. For example, Session 4 focuses on planning for explanation-driven science for a participant's curriculum—this session can be repeated multiple times over the school year for different science curriculum units. Sessions 7 and 8 focus on designing assessments and then designing the corresponding rubrics. These sessions could also be repeated multiple times over the school year, each time focusing on a different science topic (e.g., force and motion, adaptations, and erosion). The sessions can be adapted in a myriad of ways to meet the specific needs of the participants involved in the Book Study.

Table 2: Adapted Schedule of Five Meetings Each for 2.5 Hours (Total 12.5 Hours)

Session	Original Session Number	Topic
1	Session 1	Importance of supporting students in scientific explanations
	Session 2	Understanding the scientific explanation framework
	Session 3	Introducing the scientific explanation framework to students
	Homework	Read Chapters 1 and 2. Introduce the framework to students and reflect on lesson implementation.
2	Session 4	Planning for explanation-driven science
	Session 5	Scaffolding scientific talk and writing
	Homework	Read Chapters 3 and 4. Plan and teach a lesson that uses the CER framework. Design a writing scaffold and/or practice talk moves. Bring in samples of student writing and/or a video of a lesson.
3	Session 6	Instructional sequence and teaching strategies
	Homework	Read Chapter 5. Plan and teach a lesson that uses the CER framework within the instructional sequence. Adapt a teaching strategy and use it in the classroom. Bring in samples of student writing. Collect video of science teaching for final session.
4	Session 7	Designing scientific explanation assessments
	Session 8	Designing and using rubrics
	Homework	Read Chapter 6. Design and use assessment tasks with students and bring in samples of student writing.
5	Session 8	Designing and using rubrics (continue—design rubric and analyze student work)
	Session 9	Supporting learning over time
	Homework	Read Chapter 7. Develop plan for using the framework in the future.

Group Work

Throughout the sessions, the *Facilitator's Guide* suggests having the participants work in groups as they engage in different activities such as analyzing student writing, conducting science experiments, examining transcripts of classroom discussions, and designing learning tasks and assessments to try out in their classrooms. The groups should remain fairly small (e.g., four participants) to allow each member to play an active role in the discussion. When designing learning and assessment tasks, ideally participants would work with other teachers who teach the same grade and curriculum to allow them to develop a task that they can all try out in their classrooms. The participants will then be able to share student work around the same task. If this is not possible, participants can work in mixed groups and still provide feedback on each one another's learning and assessment tasks as well as student work.

The participants in the group can all teach in the same school or teach in different schools. For example, groups could include a combination of participants such as (1) four third-grade teachers each from a different school in a district; (2) two first-grade teachers from one school, and two first-grade teachers from a different school; (3) four kindergarten teachers all from one school; or (4) two second-grade teachers, one fourth-grade teacher, and one fifth-grade teacher all from one school. All of these combinations of teachers would be valuable and would offer different perspectives on how to support students in scientific explanations.

The Role of the Facilitator

The role of the facilitator is to organize the meetings, gather and prepare any materials, direct the meetings, and support the participants in developing an effective teacher community. The facilitator is not expected to be an expert on scientific explanations. Rather, the facilitator should act as a guide or a coach to support the group as a whole to develop stronger understanding and expertise over the course of the meetings. Similar to the recommendations in the book about how to support students' discussions, the facilitator should use wait time and open questions, and encourage participants to respond directly to and build on the ideas of their peers. The facilitator should encourage all participants in the group to play an active role in the community. In addition, the facilitator should be conscious of time and help the group stay on schedule to achieve all of the goals during each meeting. Following are recommendations for being an effective facilitator in terms of ways to prepare before the meetings and aspects to keep in mind during the meeting.

Recommendations to Prepare for the Meetings

- Read the entire book *What's Your Evidence? Engaging K–5 Students in Constructing Explanations in Science,* view the videos, and read the entire *Facilitator's Guide* to have an overview of the ideas and the workshop series before beginning the book group.

- Provide participants with a schedule of the workshop meetings, including the time and location for each one.

- Before the first meeting, order copies of *What's Your Evidence? Engaging K–5 Students in Constructing Explanations in Science* for all of the participants.

- Before each meeting, decide how to adapt the session or sessions to meet the needs of the participants.

- Before each meeting, gather and prepare any materials for the session (including refreshments if desired).

- Try any activities before the meeting—such as making the air bags and testing them for Session 1; analyzing students' writing using a rubric; or conducting an experiment and writing an appropriate scientific explanation.

- Send out reminders before each meeting, including a description of any homework required for that meeting.

Recommendations for Conducting the Meetings

- Start and end each session on time.

- Post or hand out an agenda that describes the activities, goals, and timeline for each meeting.

- Begin each session by reminding participants of what occurred in past meetings and describing how the goals for this meeting build on and extend the ideas discussed earlier.

- Model group norms throughout the sessions such as listening to others, being respectful, and taking risks (including acknowledging when there is something you do not know and discussing past challenges with students and how you learned from them).

- Keep the pace of each session appropriate, allowing time for idea discussion and development, but also being conscious of the overarching goals and schedule.

- Encourage all participants to be involved.

- End each meeting by providing a summary or overview of the key ideas discussed, reviewing any homework for the next session, and providing a brief overview of the goals of the next session.

Building a Community and Developing Group Norms

If the participants in the Book Study have not regularly met together as a group in the past, you may want to spend some time during the first meeting on introducing the participants, building a community, and developing group norms. Introductions can be fairly simple. For example, during the first meeting all of the participants could introduce themselves and describe the grade level they teach, the science units that are part of their curriculum, and at which school they teach.

To develop a community, lead a discussion to learn about the participants' goals for the workshops and prior experiences with students around scientific explanations. Discuss and/or post the following questions:

- What do you hope to gain from participating in the Book Study?

- Why are you interested in supporting your students in scientific explanations?

- What successes or challenges have you had in the past related to supporting students in scientific explanations?

Participants' responses to these questions can help you design and adapt future sessions to meet the needs of the participants.

To establish group norms, post and discuss group norms that all participants should keep in mind during the meetings. The group norms can help establish a community in which all participants feel safe to engage and share their ideas. A list of group norms could include ideas such as:

- Demonstrate respect for one another's ideas.

- Encourage risk taking.

- Do your best to stay on topic.

- Presume positive intentions.

- Listen to one another.

- Be open to new ideas.

- Watch your airtime to allow everyone a chance to participate.

- Come prepared and on time to all meetings.

Discuss the group norms with participants to ensure that everyone is comfortable with the environment. The participants are outstanding resources for one another and can learn so much from the feedback and ideas of their colleagues. The discussion and interaction during the Book Study can support a much more effective learning environment than reading the book in isolation. Consequently, developing a supportive community is essential to the success of the Book Study group.

Importance of Supporting Students in Scientific Explanations

Learning Objectives

1. To introduce participants to the purpose of the workshop
2. To provide a common experience that can be referred to throughout the workshop series
3. To connect writing scientific explanations to conducting investigations and collecting data
4. To assess teachers' prior knowledge about scientific explanations
5. To introduce the importance of scientific explanations

Materials

- Chart paper and markers
- Equipment and supplies for conducting the student investigation
    - A 1-gallon (nonzip) plastic bag (for each participant)
    - Masking tape
    - A plastic straw for each participant (flexible straws work well)
    - Items for testing such as:
        o Lighter-weight items (e.g., pens, markers, notebooks, etc.)
        o Heavyweight items (e.g., backpacks, laptops, dictionaries, etc.)
    - Plywood board large enough for someone to sit on (optional)
    - Copies of Handout 1—Air Bag Investigation
- Computer and LCD projector (optional)

Session Plan

Introduce the Workshop (Time: 5 minutes)

Tell participants that this workshop will focus on how to support students in constructing scientific explanations to help all children learn about the natural world and engage in scientific inquiry practices. Special attention is given to how scientific explanations help all learners develop important twenty-first-century skills that they can use not only for the science classroom, but throughout their lives. The strategies and scaffolds presented will help support all students, including English language learners (ELLs) and students with special needs, develop proficiency with this important scientific practice.

Conduct Student Investigation (Time: 40 minutes)

Tell participants they will be conducting an air bag investigation designed for elementary school students. In this investigation, they will be answering the question: *How strong is a bag of air?* The investigation is designed to be part of a larger aviation unit in which the students are investigating different properties of air, and they are about to start investigating air pressure and Bernoulli's principle. (Note: In Session 2, this investigation will be revisited. During this future session, the participants will analyze samples of strong and developing student writing using the scientific explanation framework.)

Model how to construct an air bag by inserting a straw at the top of the gallon bag. Gather the plastic around the straw and wrap a long piece of masking tape around the straw attaching it to the plastic at the top. Test the air bag to make certain that it will inflate when blown into. Show participants how to gently push on the bag so the air is expelled and they can use the air bag to test their prediction items. Pass out Handout 1—Air Bag Investigation. Before testing the air bag, have the group look around the room and select four items that they think the air bags will be able to lift and four additional items from the room that they think the air bags will not be able to lift. After the participants have written their predictions on the recording sheet, have several people share their ideas. Record some of the predictions on chart paper with a T-chart format—"Items It Will Lift" and "Items It Won't Lift"—to make a class prediction chart.

Once you have discussed predictions, have the participants test the items on their recording sheet by placing them on top of the deflated air bag and blowing into the bag to see if the item is lifted. Note that some items may roll off the bag, but that still counts as a lift. Participants should be sure to document their results on the recording sheet. The facilitator should circulate around the room encouraging participants to try heavier objects once they have tested all their items. For instance, if they have tried lifting one dictionary, encourage them to try more dictionaries and record the number they are able to lift. Ask participants if they might be able to lift a person. Encourage them to work together using a board with several bags along each edge and a person sitting in the middle.

Following the investigation with air bags, ask the participants to share their results. What surprised them about the air bags? How did their predictions match with the results? What did they notice about the bags of air? (The bags of [compressed] air were strong because they could lift heavy things.) What is their evidence that the bags of [compressed] air are strong? (They could lift laptops, dictionaries, and even a person.) What properties of air are connected to this investigation? (Air has weight. Air takes up space.)

Share Group's Scientific Explanations (Time: 20 minutes)

Have each group work together to construct a scientific explanation and write it on chart paper. Ask the groups to post their explanations around the room and describe what they wrote. *Post the following questions on a piece of chart paper or display them using an LCD projector:*

- What are the similarities and differences across what the various groups wrote?

- What are some of the characteristics of strong scientific explanations?

- What challenges do you think students have with this type of writing?

Discuss these questions as a group to develop a shared understanding of students' prior strengths and weaknesses related to scientific explanations as well as participants' goals in terms of what they would like to see their students accomplish in their writing. Keep the group explanations, as well as the answers to the previous questions, for Session 2.

Discuss Importance of Scientific Explanations (Time: 25 minutes)

Discuss and/or post the following key ideas in Chapter 1 about the importance of scientific explanations.

- Science is a social process in which scientists debate knowledge claims and continuously refine and revise knowledge based on evidence.

- Students should generate and evaluate scientific evidence and explanations.

- Scientific explanations align with reform documents focused on 21st-century skills and K–8 science classrooms.

- Scientific explanations are stressed in science education standards.

Discuss the ideas in the *National Science Education Standards* as they relate to scientific explanation and argumentation. Some of the key ideas include:

- Use data to construct a reasonable explanation (National Research Council [NRC], 1996, A: 1/4, K-4).

- Communicate investigations and explanations (NRC, 1996, A: 1/5, K-4).

- *Inquiry and the National Science Education Standards* (NRC, 2000)

    1. Engaging in scientifically oriented questions

    2. Giving priority to evidence

    3. Formulating explanations from evidence

    4. Connecting explanations to scientific knowledge

    5. Communicating and justifying explanations

The new *Framework for K–12 Science Education* (NRC, 2011) also includes a focus on scientific explanation and argumentation. For example, it states the following:

- "Early in their science education, students need opportunities to engage in constructing and critiquing explanations. They should be encouraged to develop explanations of what they observe when conducting their own investigations and to evaluate their own and others' explanations for consistency with the evidence" (pp. 3–16).

- "Young students can begin by constructing an argument for their own interpretation of the phenomena they observe and of any data they collect. They need support to go beyond simply making claims—that is, to include reasons or references to evidence and to begin to distinguish evidence from opinion" (pp. 3–19).

Extension
- Have teachers analyze their state or district standards for key ideas related to constructing scientific explanations. Discuss how these standards are similar and different compared to the national standards.

Discuss and/or post the following key benefits of engaging students in scientific explanations. This practice supports students by:

1. Providing an understanding of science concepts
2. Using evidence to support claims
3. Using logical reasoning
4. Considering and critiquing alternative explanations
5. Understanding the nature of science
6. Developing academic writing skills

This practice supports teachers by:

1. Making student thinking visible
2. Serving as an important formative and summative assessment tool

Homework

- Ask participants to read the Preface and Chapter 1.
- Have participants respond to study group question 4 in Chapter 1 before the next session.

Understanding the Scientific Explanation Framework

Learning Objectives

1. To introduce participants to the scientific explanation framework
2. To show variations in the scientific explanation framework
3. To consider what to expect with scientific explanation in elementary grades
4. To compare the difference between the terms *argument* and *explanation*

Materials

- Chart paper and markers
- Copies of Handout 2—Scientific Explanation Framework
- Copies of Handout 3—Student Writing Examples from Air Bag Investigation
- Copies of Handout 4—Variations of the Scientific Explanation Framework
- Computer and LCD projector (optional)

Session Plan

Share Homework and Introduce Learning Goals for the Day (Time: 10 minutes)

Ask participants to share the questions they recorded as part of the Session 1 homework. List the questions on chart paper as "Wonderings about Scientific Explanations." Post these questions in the room and remember to address them in subsequent discussions during the workshop.

Share with participants the learning goals for the second session. This session will introduce the scientific explanation framework as a tool for engaging students in constructing scientific explanations. Although many of the examples focus on students' written scientific explanations, the framework can also be used for classroom discussions or small-group work when students are trying to make sense of scientific data through talk.

Introduce the Scientific Explanation Framework (Time: 10 minutes)

Remind participants that science is about explaining natural phenomena, yet students can often struggle with this important scientific practice. Build off the scientific explanations that participants wrote in Session 1 for the air bag investigation. It is likely that some participants included claim or

11

evidence as part of their explanations; connect to these similarities when introducing the framework. Distribute Handout 2—Scientific Explanation Framework. Introduce the framework to the participants as a tool to help students understand how to construct a scientific explanation in both writing and talking. *Post the following definitions on a piece of chart paper or display them using an LCD projector to support the group work:*

- Claim
    - A statement that answers the question for the investigation
- Evidence
    - Scientific data that support the claim
- Reasoning
    - A justification that uses scientific principles to further explain the claim and evidence
- Rebuttal
    - Alternative explanations and counterevidence and reasoning for why the alternative is not appropriate

Show and discuss the scientific explanation framework figure (Handout 2) and discuss the definitions of each component. Stress that this is the entire framework, but it can be adapted or simplified depending on the experience and background of the students. Explain that very young students who are in kindergarten or first grade should concentrate on talking and writing about claim and evidence. Reasoning in the form of scientific principles can be added with older students as appropriate. The reasoning often includes science terms and principles that are connected with content in the lesson. Rebuttal is typically not introduced to younger or less experienced students. Different variations of the framework will be introduced and discussed later in this session.

Discuss some examples of scientific explanations identifying the different components in the examples. The examples in Table 2.1 in Chapter 2 can be used to illustrate these different components. Participants can either look at the table in the book or post the examples on a piece of chart paper or display them using an LCD projector. Discuss differences in the evidence in the examples such as the use of qualitative versus quantitative evidence. Discuss differences in the complexity of the reasoning, such as how the life science example about bush plants is fairly simple in explaining why the evidence supports the claim, while the physical science example includes more complex reasoning that includes the scientific principle of kinetic energy.

Extension
- Have teachers analyze the student activities in one chapter or section in their current science curriculum. Ask teachers to identify which activities would and would not be appropriate to ask students to construct a scientific explanation (e.g., there is evidence available to support a claim).

Analyze Student Writing from Air Bag Experiment (Time: 30 minutes)

Remind participants of the air bag experiment from Session 1. Distribute the four examples of students' work from the air bag experiments (Handout 3). Have participants work in groups to analyze the samples of student work and look for common difficulties in writing scientific explanations. *Post the following directions on a piece of chart paper or display them using an LCD projector:*

- With your group, analyze the fourth-grade students' writing:

  1. Analyze each student's writing in terms of claim, evidence, and reasoning.

  2. Rank the students' examples from 1 (being the strongest) to 4 (being the weakest).

     - Why did you rank #1 the strongest?

     - What challenges did students have?

  3. If you gave this learning task to your students, what challenges do you think they would have? Why?

After the groups finish analyzing the student work, discuss the student examples. Take a poll (and perhaps write it on chart paper or display using an LCD projector) on how the groups ranked Students A, B, C, and D. Typically, participants will rank Student B as the strongest (#1) and Student A as the weakest (#4) with Students C and D in the middle.

Ask participants: What are the strengths of Student C's response? Discuss these strengths, such as the student includes detailed evidence that supports the claim and two scientific principles about the properties of air that are connected with the investigation. Ask participants: What challenges did the students have in their writing? Discuss these challenges such as (1) vague evidence (Student A); (2) not enough evidence (Student A); and (3) vague reasoning (Students A and C).

Ask participants how this student writing is similar to and different from what they would expect of their own students. Discuss challenges that their students have with scientific explanation.

Share What to Expect in Elementary Grades (Time: 10 minutes)

Address that while younger students are excellent thinkers and can readily begin to construct claims from their observations, as well as appropriately use the language of evidence, it is not until students are older that they are ready to participate in some of the more complex aspects of this practice, such as applying scientific principles and suggesting and/or critiquing alternative explanations. Discuss and/or post the following points:

- The connection among question–claim–evidence is the most basic form of scientific explanation and is suitable for all grade levels.

- As early as kindergarten, students can begin to use the term *evidence* when talking about their observations.

- As students tackle more substantial science content in grades 3 to 5, it is reasonable to consider having them use science principles to justify connections between claim and evidence.

- Identifying and critiquing alternative explanations is more common among older students. This aspect of scientific explanation is quite sophisticated and not often observed in students' writing and talking.

- Science notebooks:

  - Science notebooks are a useful way for students to document their tests, observations/data, and thinking over time.

  - During science talks in which students are constructing explanations, encourage them to bring their science notebooks with them and to refer to them during the discussion, especially when proposing evidence to support a claim.

- Even kindergarten children can develop meaningful notebook entries that use drawings and simple phrases to document their observations.

Connect these points to the discussion of the four student responses from the air bag experiment as well as other student examples the participants introduced from their own classrooms.

Discuss the Difference between Explanation and Argumentation (Time: 10 minutes)

Tell participants that there is debate in the science education community about whether to refer to the claim, evidence, and reasoning (CER) framework as a "scientific explanation" or as a "scientific argument." Discuss and/or post the following key ideas:

- An **explanation** *makes sense* of how or why a phenomenon occurred. Two examples follow:
  - Explain why the biodiversity decreased.
  - Explain what has happened to the pitch of bird songs in cities.
- An **argument** *defends or supports* knowledge claims through evidence, warrants, and backing. Two examples follow:
  - Argue for your explanation for why the biodiversity decreased.
  - Argue for your experimental design to study what is happening to the biodiversity.

The CER framework combines the goals of both explanation and argumentation. The framework asks students to explain a phenomenon and to use evidence and reasoning to defend or support that explanation. The CER framework is a tool that should be adapted by participants to support their students. It can be referred to as the scientific explanation framework, scientific argumentation framework, or CER framework depending on what participants feel is appropriate for their students. Ask participants what language they think would work best with their students and why.

Show and Discuss Variation of the Scientific Explanation Framework (Time: 20 minutes)

Pass out Handout 4—Variations of the Scientific Explanation Framework. Describe the four variations. Ask participants why a teacher may decide to use one variation compared to another with their students.

Ask participants to work in small groups to identify which variation was used in the air bag investigation from Session 1. Ask participants to discuss how to modify the activity so that it would include other variations of the framework (both simpler and more complex).

After discussing the air bag investigation with their small groups, have the participants reconvene as a whole group and share their ideas. Discuss the current variation of the framework used in the air bag investigation (i.e., Variation #3—Evidence includes multiple pieces and reasoning includes a justification). Have participants share their ideas about how to modify the activity.

Homework

- Ask participants to read Chapter 2.

Introducing the Scientific Explanation Framework to Students

Learning Objectives

1. To review the scientific explanation framework
2. To illustrate how to introduce the scientific explanation framework to students
3. To design a lesson on how to introduce the scientific explanation framework

Materials

- Chart paper and markers
- Copies of Handout 4—Variations of the Scientific Explanation Framework
- Video 2.1—Introducing the CER Framework
- Computer (with speakers) and LCD projector

Session Plan

Introduce the Learning Goals and Review the CER Framework (Time: 10 minutes)

Briefly share with participants the learning goals for this session. This session will review the different components of the scientific explanation framework and illustrate how to discuss the framework with students through the use of a video clip from a third-grade elementary teacher and her students. Post the definitions of the different components of the scientific explanation framework from Session 2 either on large chart paper or using an LCD projector. Ask participants if there are any questions about the different components of the framework or ideas about the components that the participants would like to share after reading Chapter 2 in the book.

Watch and Discuss Video of Ms. Hershberger Introducing the CER Framework (Time: 35 minutes)

Tell participants that they will be watching and discussing the video clip of the third-grade teacher introducing the three parts of the scientific explanation framework to her students. Remind participants that this video clip occurs midway through the school year and takes place during a unit on simple machines. The students have been writing claims and evidence as part of their science notebooks for several months, and Ms. Hershberger has just introduced the idea of scientific reasoning.

Ms. Hershberger wants to review the framework and make a poster that can be displayed in the classroom to remind students of the different components of an explanation. Tell participants that the whole video clip is about 5 minutes long and ask them to listen for student thinking. Play video 2.1—Introducing the CER Framework.

Ask participants questions to reflect on both what is occurring in Ms. Hershberger's classroom as well as how they might apply or adapt the strategies she uses to their own classrooms. Focus on the relevant components of claim, evidence, and reasoning. Ask questions such as:

- What parts of the framework are the students familiar with already?

- What are the students' ideas about the components?

- What difficulties are the third-graders having with discussing the words *claim* and *evidence*? (They keep trying to provide specific claims and evidence instead of generalizing about the terms.)

- What materials did Ms. Hershberger ask her students to bring to the discussion? (They have recording sheets from an investigation with a question at the top and a data chart.)

- How similar or different do you think your students' ideas would be compared to Ms. Hershberger's third-grade students? Why?

- What strategies do you think you might use to introduce the framework to your students? How would this be similar to and different from Ms. Hershberger's classroom? Why?

During the discussion, encourage participants to reflect on some of the strategies that Ms. Hershberger uses such as (1) eliciting students' prior ideas about how to justify or support ideas in science and the definitions of the different terms; (2) recording the final definitions of the components on the board; and (3) using the students' recording sheet to help them think about the parts of an explanation.

Design a Lesson on How to Introduce the Scientific Explanation Framework (Time: 30 minutes)

Tell participants that they will be working in groups to design a lesson in which they will be introducing the scientific explanation framework to their students and asking students to write their first scientific explanation. (Note: Teachers of younger students may want to introduce the terms *claim* and *evidence* as part of the lesson. For example, the question for the investigation could be introduced at the beginning of the lesson and then the teacher could use a chart or recording sheet with the words *claim* and *evidence* as they discuss the results of the lesson in a group science talk. When the words *claim* and *evidence* are introduced in the context of an investigation, younger students are better able to understand their meaning.)

In designing the lesson and recording sheet, the participants should consider places in their current curriculum where students collect either observational or numerical data. It is essential that students have data, because they need to be able to support their claims with evidence. Remind the participants of the four variations of the framework discussed in Session 2 and ask them to take out their copies of Handout 4—Variations of the Scientific Explanation Framework. In designing the introductory lesson, participants will also need to decide what variation of the framework to use initially with their students.

Tell participants that they will try this lesson before the next meeting and share with their group to reflect on the successes and challenges of the lesson. Suggest that participants keep in mind what they will be doing in their classrooms before the next meeting. *Post the following directions about designing the introductory lesson on a piece of chart paper or display them using an LCD projector:*

- Each group should record on chart paper:
    1. Variation of the framework (see Handout 4)
    2. Question students will respond to (make sure it requires evidence)
    3. Example of an ideal student response with claim and evidence (and if applicable, reasoning)
    4. Description of any strategies (e.g., visual representations, everyday examples)

Share and Critique Lessons (Time: 15 minutes)

Have the groups post their introductory lessons on the walls around the room. Ask each group to share their introductory lesson. After sharing the lesson, other groups can ask questions or provide feedback. Discuss all of the lessons as a group. Ask questions such as:

- What variation of the framework was most common across the different groups? Why?
- After listening to the different groups, does anyone have any new ideas about how they might introduce the framework to their students? If yes, what are they?
- What do you think will be most challenging for your students?
- Do you have any remaining questions about how to introduce the framework?

Homework

- Ask participants to introduce the scientific explanation framework to their students before the next session.

Planning for Explanation-Driven Science

Learning Objectives

1. To further enhance comprehension of the scientific explanation framework by sharing introductory lessons with peers

2. To build capability for developing a coherent content storyline and designing scientific explanation learning tasks

3. To design a lesson that uses the CER framework to try in the classroom

Materials

- Chart paper and markers
- Copies of Handout 5—Planning for Scientific Explanation
- Computer and LCD projector (optional)

Session Plan

Introduce the Learning Goals for the Day (Time: 5 minutes)

Briefly share with participants the learning goals for the fourth session. This session will explore how to design lessons to support students in constructing scientific explanations. This process begins by identifying places in your curriculum that provide opportunities for scientific explanations. Then you will consider how you can modify tasks to varying degrees of complexity to meet the needs of your students. Finally, you will consider how elements of a coherent content storyline will ensure your lesson is connected to science ideas in ways that make it more understandable to students.

Share and Discuss Introductory CER Framework Lessons (Time: 30 minutes)

Begin by asking participants to describe their experiences introducing the scientific explanation framework since the last session. *Post the following direction and discussion questions on a piece of chart paper or display them using an LCD projector to support the group work:*

- How did you introduce CER?
- What went well during the lesson?
- What challenges arose?
- What did you learn that you hope to address or apply in your next CER lesson?

After the groups share and discuss their lessons, reconvene as a whole group. Discuss and/or post the following questions:

- What were some ways of introducing the scientific explanation framework that were effective? Why were they effective?

- What did you learn from your discussion with your colleagues?

- What remaining questions do you have?

Introduce the Process of Designing a Scientific Explanation Learning Task (Time: 15 minutes)

Introduce participants to the process of designing a scientific explanation learning task. There are four main steps: (1) specify a learning goal and identify opportunities in the curriculum that provide opportunities to write scientific explanations; (2) design the complexity of the task; (3) use the planning matrix to craft a scientific explanation sequence; and (4) examine the learning task for coherence. Distribute Handout 5—Planning for Scientific Explanation. Each step is briefly described as follows. Discuss each of these steps as the participants follow along on the handout. It can be helpful to work through a common lesson, such as air bags, as an example of each step in context.

Step 1: Specify the Learning Goal

    a. Specify your learning goal. (See Figure 3.2 from the text.)

        i. Describe what you want students to be able to "do" with their science knowledge. In this case, construct a scientific explanation.

        ii. Develop a *learning performance* by combining both the science content and the scientific inquiry practice to specify what students should be able to do. In this case, students should construct a scientific explanation.

    b. Identify opportunities in the curriculum that contain scientific data needed for the evidence part of CER.

        i. Recognize that engaging in scientific explanation requires identifying places in the curriculum or designing activities when students engage with phenomena, collect data, and make sense of it.

        ii. Provide opportunities for students to have access to data they can use as evidence to support a claim. While it is not always necessary for students to collect data themselves, when working with younger children it is desirable for them to collect data firsthand. Consider how you will help young students view their observations as data in cases where numerical data are not available.

    c. Identify the scientific principles students will use.

        i. Recognize that constructing scientific explanations necessarily focuses on a science idea. The learning task needs to align with the scientific principles you want students to learn.

        ii. Provide opportunities for older students to be able to apply one or more scientific principles that show why the data count as evidence to support the claim.

Step 2: Design the Complexity of the Learning Task (see Figure 3.1 from the text)

    a. Attend to the openness of the question.

        i. Consider how open or closed you want the question to be.

  b. Vary the complexity and type of data.

   i. Consider both quantitative (such as measurements) and qualitative data (such as observations).

  c. Vary the amount of data.

   i. Select the variation of the scientific explanation framework (simple to complex) that you will use (see Handout 4).

Step 3: Use the Planning Matrix

  a. Develop a claim.

   i. Your claim should be based on the learning performance you developed in step 1a.

   ii. The claim should be worded using language that the students in your class are likely to propose.

  b. Craft a question.

   i. Keep in mind that the claim must answer this question.

   ii. Attend to the openness of the question from step 2a.

  c. Specify evidence and activities.

   i. For each claim in the sequence, specify the data that will be used as evidence to construct the claim. Consider the type and amount of data from steps 2b and 2c.

   ii. Briefly describe the activities students will do to generate the data.

  d. Integrate scientific reasoning.

   i. Revisit the scientific principles you identified in step 1c.

   ii. Use the scientific principles to justify the connection between evidence and claim.

Step 4: Examine the Learning Task for Coherence

  a. Consider the main elements of a coherent content storyline.

   i. If you have followed this process, your learning task should reflect one main science idea (consistent with the learning goal); use a focus question that is aligned with the learning goal; and engage students in activities that generate appropriate evidence related to the main science idea.

  b. Make other considerations.

   i. Coherence also includes other elements. Consider the following questions: *If there is more than one activity, are they sequenced appropriately? If you are using other representations, such as analogies, diagrams, and models, are they matched to the main science idea? How will you synthesize the key ideas of the lesson? How can the science ideas from this learning task be linked to other content ideas in the unit?*

Design a Scientific Explanation Learning Task (Time: 30 minutes)

Have participants work in groups to design a scientific explanation learning task by (1) specifying a learning goal and identifying opportunities in the curriculum that provide opportunities to write scientific explanations; (2) designing the complexity of the task; (3) using the planning matrix to craft a scientific explanation sequence; and (4) examining the learning task for coherence. Have participants use Handout 5—Planning for Scientific Explanation to create the content storyline and learning tasks for a lesson or sequence of lessons that they will teach.

Share and Critique Lessons (Time: 10 minutes)

Have each group share their learning tasks with others. Have participants ask questions and provide feedback on various aspects of the learning task to each group. The following questions can be used to guide feedback:

- Does the lesson have an appropriate learning goal?

- Does the lesson use data from the curriculum? Are the data appropriate?

- Is the level of complexity of the data appropriate? Why or why not?

- Is the variation of the CER framework appropriate?

- Which elements of a coherent content storyline are reflected in the learning task?

After discussing each group's work, ask participants if they have any other comments or questions about either designing or trying out this lesson in their classrooms.

Extension

- If participants can meet more than eight times, the activity of designing learning tasks can be repeated multiple times during the school year. Participants can use the planning matrix to design a coherent content storyline for an entire unit or units in the curriculum. These storylines can also be provided to other teachers in the district to be used in their classrooms. For example, a website can be developed with all of the learning tasks.

Homework

- Ask participants to read Chapter 3.

- Ask participants to teach the lesson they designed with their students before the next session. Participants should bring copies of student work (e.g., six students—two stronger, two middle, and two weaker) to share with their group and discuss at the next session.

Scaffolding Scientific Talk and Writing

Learning Objectives

1. To analyze students' written scientific explanations and assess strengths and weaknesses
2. To introduce (a) talk moves for supporting scientific discourse and (b) characteristics and structures for writing scaffolds
3. To design a writing scaffold for supporting students in constructing a scientific explanation and implement it in the classroom

Materials

- Chart paper and markers
- Copies of Handout 6—Battery and Bulb Lesson Transcript
- Copies of Handout 7—Writing Scaffold for Adaptation Investigation
- Video 4.2—Talk Moves
- Computer (with speakers) and LCD projector

Session Plan

Introduce the Learning Goals for the Day (Time: 5 minutes)

Briefly share with participants the learning goals for Session 5. This session will explore the interplay between talking and writing in the process of constructing scientific explanations. Participants will be introduced to scaffolding for whole-class and small-group talk, as well as to writing scaffolds. Structures for writing scaffolds will be discussed, such as explanations, sentence starters, and questions. Finally, approaches such as creating visual representations of the CER framework to post in the classroom will be introduced.

Share and Discuss Student Writing (Time: 20 minutes)

Tell participants that they will be returning to their small groups from the last session in which they designed a learning task incorporating the CER framework. In their groups, the participants should share the samples of student writing and discuss the strengths and challenges of the lesson. *Post the following discussion questions on a piece of chart paper or display them using an LCD projector:*

- What went well during the lesson?

- What challenges arose?

- What were the strengths and weaknesses of your students' writing?

- What did you learn that you hope to address or apply in your next lesson that includes scientific explanations?

After each small group has shared and discussed its lesson, reconvene the whole group to discuss different lessons learned. Discuss and/or post the following questions:

- What did you learn that you hope to address or apply in your next scientific explanation lesson?

- What were the challenges and successes?

- What did you learn from your discussion with your colleagues?

- What remaining questions do you have?

Emphasize that constructing strong scientific explanations takes time. The students need to become familiar with the framework and learn how to justify the claims they are making in both discussions and in their writing. In order to support students with this challenging task, there are a variety of different supports that you can use.

Introduce Talk Scaffolds and Watch Video (Time: 20 minutes)

Explain to participants that scaffolds are supports that are designed to help learners engage in activities that they would be unable to accomplish without them, and that students also learn from interacting with scaffolds. Refer participants to Table 4.1 from the text and distribute Handout 6—Battery and Bulb Lesson Transcript (for video clip 4.2). Tell participants that talk moves can be used effectively to scaffold class discussion focused on building scientific explanations. After reviewing the talk moves (e.g., re-voicing, asking students to apply their own reasoning, asking students to explicate their reasoning), watch video clip 4.2. Have participants analyze the transcript for talk moves. Discuss the following questions:

- What did you notice about the class discussion in terms of the role of the teacher and student participation?

- How did Ms. Hershberger use the talk moves?

- What makes the talk moves unique to science? (Address the focus on evidence and what counts as evidence.)

Have participants consider how supporting students' small-group talk differs from whole-class discussion. Note that teachers often attend to small groups by asking students about what they are doing rather than what sense they are making. Using the strategies in the book can help shift the focus to sense making. Discuss three ways in which teachers can interact with small groups to support explanation building.

- Use the CER Framework—Refer participants to Table 4.2. Consider how the CER framework can be used to refocus students on the guiding question, encourage students to examine the data for patterns, attempt to draft a claim using evidence, consider alternative explanations, and make predictions using previously developed explanations.

- Monitor and Assess Student Thinking—Share the example from the text in which young children consider bigger numbers to be better in the context of a question about pendulums. Discuss examples from participants' classrooms in which they uncovered children struggling to make sense of a science idea by visiting and talking with small groups.

- Encourage Participation—Explain that students who are reluctant to share in whole-group discussion can be encouraged to participate during small group. Listen for and record important contributions you hear in small-group discussion. Attribute those ideas to particular students during whole-group discussion, or ask students to repeat their contribution in this setting.

Introduce and Design Supports for Scientific Writing (Time: 30 minutes)

As you introduce supports for scientific writing, participants may want to know whether it makes a difference to engage students in talking before writing or vice versa. Explain to the participants that talking and writing scientific explanations are complementary activities. For young or inexperienced learners, it is important to talk before writing so that the class can practice sharing data and looking for patterns, as well as constructing claims from evidence. Once students have experience with co-constructing scientific explanations, they can engage in aspects of writing explanations independently or in small groups and then bring that work to the whole-class discussion.

Refer participants to Table 4.3 and discuss the four characteristics of writing scaffolds: (1) general and content support, (2) detail and length, (3) fading, and (4) structure. Distribute Handout 7—Writing Scaffold for Adaptation Investigation—and use it to illustrate these characteristics. Have participants mark up the writing scaffold. For example, under "Evidence" it says: *Provide scientific data to support your claim. The evidence should include the amount of food (marbles, pennies, popsicle sticks, and red water) that the bird ate.* The first part of the prompt is general support for the scientific explanation framework, while the second part of the prompt is content-specific support unique to the adaptation investigation.

Refer participants to Table 4.4 and discuss the three structures for writing scaffolds: (1) explanation, (2) sentence starters, and (3) questions. Put participants into small groups and have them design a writing scaffold that they can use in their classrooms.

Share Writing Scaffolds (Time: 15 minutes)

Have each group share their writing scaffolds. After sharing the scaffolds, other groups can ask questions or provide feedback. Discuss all of the writing scaffolds as a whole group. Ask questions such as:

- Which writing scaffolds do you think will be most useful to the students in your classroom?

- How can we modify writing scaffolds for use with kindergarten students?

- Other than time constraints, what do you think will be challenging about integrating the writing scaffolds into your science teaching?

Homework

- Ask participants to read Chapter 4.

- Have participants create a visual representation of the CER framework for their class.

- Option A: Ask participants to video record themselves enacting a science talk. They should then watch the video and select a two- to three-minute section to share with the group at the next session.

- Option B: Ask participants to use the writing scaffold they designed in class with students. They should bring copies of student work (e.g., samples from six students—two stronger, two average, and two developing) to share with their group and discuss at the next session.

Instructional Sequence and Teaching Strategies

Learning Objectives

1. To analyze students' written scientific explanations and assess strengths and weaknesses

2. To examine science talk videos for use of talk moves for supporting scientific explanation

3. To introduce the instructional sequence and teaching strategies for supporting scientific explanations

4. To design a lesson that follows the instructional sequence and includes one of the teaching strategies for scientific explanation

Materials

- Chart paper and markers
- Copies of Handout 8—Instructional Sequence for Constructing Scientific Explanations
- Copies of Handout 9—Integrate Instructional Sequence for Constructing Scientific Explanations
- Videos 5.1 to 5.8
- Computer (with speakers) and LCD projector

Session Plan

Introduce the Learning Goals for the Day (Time: 5 minutes)

Briefly share with participants the learning goals for Session 6. In this session, participants will have an opportunity to analyze their science talk videos and samples of students' written explanations. They will be introduced to the instructional sequence for constructing scientific explanations, as well as to instructional strategies for engaging students in scientific explanation. These strategies include using the KLEW(S) chart, critiquing a sample explanation, and debating a peer explanation. Finally, participants will have an opportunity to work together to plan a lesson using the instructional sequence and include one of the teaching strategies.

Share and Discuss Science Talk Videos and Student Writing Samples (Time: 20 minutes)

Tell participants that they will be returning to their small groups from the last session in which they designed a writing scaffold to use in their classrooms. In their groups, the participants should share the samples of student writing and discuss the strengths and challenges of the lesson. Those participants who video recorded a science talk should be given the opportunity to share and discuss those in small groups, as well. *Post the following discussion questions on a piece of chart paper or display them using an LCD projector:*

- What went well during your science talk? What challenges arose? How did the talk moves that you used support students' discussion and explanation building?

- What were the strengths and weaknesses of your students' writing? How did the writing scaffold that you developed support students' explanation writing?

- What did you learn that you hope to address or apply in your next lesson that includes scientific explanations?

After each small group has shared and discussed its lesson, reconvene the whole group to discuss different lessons learned. Discuss and/or post the following questions:

- What did you learn that you hope to address or apply in your next scientific explanation lesson?

- What were the challenges and successes?

- What did you learn from your discussion with your colleagues?

- What remaining questions do you have?

Emphasize that constructing strong scientific explanations takes time. Students need to become familiar with the framework and learn how to support (and justify) the claims they are making in both discussions and in their writing. In order to support students with this challenging scientific practice, there are a variety of different strategies that you can use.

Watch and Discuss Videos of the Instructional Sequence and Teaching Strategies (Time: 30 minutes)

Pass out Handout 8—Instructional Sequence for Constructing Scientific Explanations to the participants. Tell the participants that they will be watching videos of elementary school teachers using each of these strategies with their own students in K–5 classrooms. The instructional sequence is an ideal progression for engaging students in building explanations from evidence, especially when there are opportunities to collect firsthand data. In those cases where older students are provided with secondary source data, the sequence can be adapted. The handout is provided to record any comments or notes as the videos are shown and discussed.

In Video 5.1 the lesson has been edited together to illustrate all of the components of the complete instructional sequence. Each component of the sequence has one video example on the DVD in Chapter 5. Show Video 5.1 to introduce the components. If time allows, you can ask the participants if there are other sequence components that they would like to see.

Sequence Component	Description	Video
Assessing prior knowledge	Find out what students *think* they know about the big idea you will be investigating.	5.2—What We Think We Know
Framing the question	Introduce students to the question that will drive the investigation.	No video
Making predictions	Get students to make a commitment about what they think will happen during the investigation. This can be another way of assessing prior knowledge.	5.3—Making Predictions
Collecting, recording, and interpreting data	Provide students with an opportunity to test their predictions, collect and record data/observations, and represent and make sense of the data (e.g., create a graph, identify patterns).	5.4—Data Collection
Constructing a scientific explanation	Use the evidence to create a statement that answers the question (i.e., claim). Integrate reasoning to further develop the relationship between claim and evidence.	5.5—Claim from Evidence

In video 5.1, discuss how Ms. Hershberger included each of the components of the sequence in her lesson. Point out that although many teachers have their students participate in hands-on activities, few press for making sense of the data in the larger context of the science idea. The instructional sequence emphasizes collecting data with purpose and follows through on having students construct a claim using the evidence from the activity/investigation. Throughout the process priority is given to students' ideas and thinking.

Explain to participants that there are several teaching strategies that can be used to enhance components of the instructional sequence. Briefly introduce the strategies addressed in Chapter 5.

- Introduce the CER Framework—This is similar to what participants learned in Session 3. However, the example provided in the text suggests using a nonscience example that students are likely to be interested in, such as "Justin Bieber is the best musician that ever lived." Starting with this kind of claim provides a context for students to consider what counts as evidence and how to craft a claim that is appropriate given the type and amount of available data.

- Use the KLEW(S) Chart—A KLEW(S) chart is an explanation mapping strategy that can be used throughout a lesson or unit of study for students to document their prior knowledge, data from investigations, claims developed from those data, scientific principles that can be used to justify the claim–evidence relationship, and wonderings/questions that arise. Refer participants to Table 5.2 and Figure 5.1 in the text. Video clip 5.6 shows Ms. Hershberger's class examining data for patterns and then constructing a claims and transferring it to the KLEW(S) chart.

- Critique a Sample Explanation—This strategy involves the teacher providing multiple-choice possibilities for claim and evidence during a science talk. Students must select the best option and then justify their choice. Video clip 5.7 from Ms. Hershberger's class demonstrates this strategy in action.

- Debate a Peer Explanation—This strategy requires students to work in their small groups to draft explanations, which are presented to the class. When different claims exist among groups, the discussion can be framed as a debate based on evidence. However, when students have variations of the same explanation, they can critique one another's explanation until they co-construct one that is acceptable to the class. See video clip 5.8 for an example of this strategy.

After introducing each teaching strategy, ask the teachers to reflect on it and how it might be used in their own classrooms. Ask questions such as:

- What is the value of this teaching strategy?
- How could you use the strategy in your own teaching?

After introducing all of the strategies, have the teachers reflect on which strategies they may want to integrate into their teaching. Ask questions such as:

- Which strategies would you use in your teaching?
- Would some of the strategies work better at different times of the year? If yes, why?

Design a Lesson Using the Instructional Sequence for Constructing Explanations (Time: 30 minutes)

Have teachers work in small groups to plan a lesson using the instructional sequence. Distribute Handout 9—Integrate Instructional Sequence for Constructing Scientific Explanations for participants to use while they plan. Remind them to begin with the planning process described in Session 4. More specifically, they should specify a learning goal based on a science idea, and then design a question for which students can construct a claim from evidence. They should write out an ideal student response to the question that includes all aspects of a scientific explanation appropriate for the learners (claim and evidence for younger students; claim, evidence, and reasoning for older, more experienced learners). Finally, teachers should integrate the instructional sequence to support the development of the scientific explanation they are attempting to build with students. As an extension, encourage teachers to include one of the teaching strategies introduced in this session.

After designing the instructional sequence, participants should record their ideas on large chart paper. *Post the following directions on a piece of chart paper or display them using an LCD projector:*

Each group should record on chart paper:

1. Question for the learning task
2. Example of an ideal student response with claim, evidence, and reasoning
3. Description of the instructional sequence and teaching strategy

Share Teaching Strategies (Time: 20 minutes)

Have the groups post their instructional sequences and teaching strategies on the walls around the room. Ask each group to share their lesson. After each group shares, other groups can ask questions or provide feedback. Discuss all of the instructional sequences as a group. Ask questions such as:

- Other than time constraints, what do you think will be challenging about integrating the instructional sequence into your classroom?

- What teaching strategies intrigue you that you might consider using in your classroom?

Extension
- If participants can meet more than eight times, this session can be broken into two—one session on the instructional sequence and another session on teaching strategies.

Homework

- Ask participants to read Chapter 5.

- Ask participants to video record their teaching during a part of the instructional sequence in which the class is engaged in discussion and using the scientific explanation framework. They should then watch the video and select a two- to three-minute video clip to share at the final session. The video clip will be examined to reflect on the role of the framework in discussions, the interactions between the students, and the role of the teacher in supporting classroom discussions.

Designing Scientific Explanation Assessments

Learning Objectives

1. To introduce a development process for designing scientific explanation assessment tasks

2. To design an assessment task in which students provide a claim and support it with evidence (and, if applicable, reasoning and rebuttal)

Materials

- Chart paper and markers
- Copies of Handout 10—Designing Assessment Tasks—Force and Motion Example
- Copies of Handout 11—Designing Assessment Tasks
- Access to district, state, or national standards (i.e., paper copies or Internet access)
- Computer and LCD projector (optional)

Session Plan

Discuss Development Process for Assessment Tasks (Time: 20 minutes)

Tell participants that the focus will now shift to discussing how to design assessment tasks. The scientific explanation framework can be used to support students' writing and talk during science investigations and other classroom activities as well as when writing responses to more summative assessments. The design process for developing assessment tasks is similar to developing learning tasks, which was discussed in Session 4. *Post the following five steps of the assessment design process on a piece of chart paper or display them using an LCD projector:*

- Step 1: Identify and unpack the content standards.
- Step 2: Select scientific explanation level of complexity.
- Step 3: Create learning performance.
- Step 4: Write the assessment task.
- Step 5: Develop specific rubric.

Tell participants that in this session they will focus on the first four steps to design the assessment task. They will then try the assessment task and collect student writing or student talk (e.g., podcasts, video-recorded presentations, etc.) before the next workshop session. At the next workshop session, they will design a rubric for the assessment task.

Discuss steps 1–4 with the participants. Pass out Handout 10—Designing Assessment Tasks— Force and Motion Example. This example is from Chapter 6 in the book and focuses on developing a writing assessment for fourth-grade students that is a formative assessment in conjunction with an investigation. Describe the example and explain each step that goes along with it. After discussing the example, ask if there are any questions about it or the different steps. If you are focusing on student talk, younger students, or summative assessments, you may also want to discuss how the example could look different for your specific focus.

Design Assessment Tasks (Time: 45 minutes)

Pass out Handout 11—Designing Assessment Tasks. Ask participants to work in groups and use the handout to develop an assessment task that they can use with their students before the next session. Participants should work through all four steps in the assessment development design process. They should use other resources (either books or the Internet) to identify an appropriate standard. Furthermore, they can search online to find common student misconceptions about the science topic.

After completing the design of the assessment task, the participants should record on large chart paper (1) the content standard and (2) the assessment task.

Share Assessment Tasks (Time: 15 minutes)

Have the groups post their assessment tasks on the walls around the room. Ask groups to describe the process they went through to design their assessment tasks and to share their assessment tasks. After each group presents, have the other participants ask questions and provide any suggestions on how to improve the assessment. Have the groups discuss if they want to make any revisions to the assessment before trying the assessment task with their students.

Discuss Design Process (Time: 10 minutes)

Discuss as a whole group the entire design process for the assessment tasks. Ask questions such as:

- What challenges arose as you were designing the assessment tasks?

- How are these assessments similar and different compared to assessments you have designed in the past? Compared to other assessments (such as state assessments) that students take?

Extension
- If participants can meet more than eight times, the activity of designing assessment tasks can be repeated multiple times during the school year. Participants can design assessment tasks for different units in the curriculum. These assessment tasks can also be provided to other teachers in the district to be used in their classrooms. For example, a website can be developed with all of the assessment tasks.

Homework

- Ask participants to read Chapter 6.
- Ask participants to use the assessment task with their students before the next session. Participants should bring copies of student work (e.g., six students—two stronger, two average, and two developing) to share with their group and discuss at the next session.

SESSION 8 Designing and Using Rubrics

Learning Goals

1. To analyze students' scientific explanations for strengths and weaknesses using a specific rubric

2. To design specific rubrics for assessments and learning tasks

3. To provide students with feedback on their scientific explanations that support student learning

Materials

- Chart paper and markers
- Copies of Handout 12—Base Scientific Explanation Rubric
- Copies of Handout 13—Specific Scientific Explanation Rubric—How Does the Position of the Light Source Change the Position of the Shadow?
- Copies of Handout 14—Student Examples—How Does the Position of the Light Source Change the Position of the Shadow?
- Copies of Handout 15—Student Examples—What Happens When You Mix Solids?
- Computer and LCD projector (optional)

Session Plan

Discuss Development Process for Specific Rubrics (Time: 15 minutes)

Tell participants that this session will focus on the design and use of rubrics to support student learning and inform instruction. Scientific explanation assessment tasks can be used as (1) summative assessments—cumulative assessments that capture the quality of student learning and judge performance against some standard; and (2) formative assessments—assessments that provide information to teachers and students that are used to improve teaching and learning. Rubrics can allow you to assess students' strengths and weaknesses with scientific explanations to evaluate both students' performance as well as to inform your instruction to better meet their needs.

Discuss how to develop a specific rubric by adapting a base rubric for scientific explanation. Tell participants that this process can be used to develop rubrics both for assessment tasks and for learning tasks. Pass out Handout 12—Base Scientific Explanation Rubric. Discuss the base scientific rubric with the participants. The rubric contains four different components—claim, evidence,

34

reasoning, and rebuttal. For each component, there are multiple levels depending on the design of the learning task or the assessment task. For example, one task may require two pieces of evidence in which case there would be three levels—0, 1, and 2—while another task may require four pieces of evidence in which case there would be five levels—0, 1, 2, 3, and 4.

Tell participants that to adapt the base rubric to develop a specific rubric for an assessment or learning task it can be helpful to write an ideal student response for that question. The ideal student response illustrates the desired outcome for the quantity of the components (i.e., Will it include reasoning or a rebuttal?) and the complexity of the components (i.e., How many pieces of evidence should the students include?). The base rubric and the ideal student response can then be used to create a specific rubric.

Pass out Handout 13—Specific Scientific Explanation Rubric—How Does the Position of the Light Source Change the Position of the Shadow? Tell participants that this rubric was developed for a learning task for third-grade students who conducted an investigation using a pipe cleaner person and a flashlight to investigate how the position of a light source changes the position of the shadow. In this case, the teacher asked the students to justify their claim with evidence and reasoning, but they were not asked to include a rebuttal. Discuss the different components and levels of the rubrics with the participants.

Analyze Samples of Student Writing Using Specific Rubric (Time: 30 minutes)

Pass out Handout 14—Student Examples—How Does the Position of the Light Source Change the Position of the Shadow? Ask participants to work in their groups to analyze samples of third-graders' writing using the specific rubric. *Post the following directions on a piece of chart paper or display them using an LCD projector:*

- Score the four student responses using the specific rubric. For each student give them a separate score for:

  - Claim: 0, 1, or 2

  - Evidence: 0, 1, 2, or 3

  - Reasoning: 0, 1, or 2

- Provide feedback and strategies

  - What feedback would you provide this student? Why would that feedback be helpful?

  - What strategies might you use to help this student construct a stronger explanation?

After each group finishes evaluating the student responses, discuss what score they provided each student for each component. You may want to tally the participants' scores on a piece of chart paper or have each group record its score on chart paper and post it on the walls of the room. For any student responses where there are disagreements in scores, discuss with the participants why they decided to give a student a particular score. Emphasize that it is challenging to score students' writing and there are often gray areas. For example, we debated whether to give Student A a 1 or 2 for reasoning because the student said "it" blocked the light. We decided we wanted him or her to be more specific (e.g., pipe cleaner person or object) so we gave the student the lower score. Overall we have found that the more specific the rubric, the easier it is to come to agreement.

Student Example	Score
Student A	
When the light moves, the shadow moves the opposite way.	Claim—1
When we shine the light on the left side of the shadow, it is on the opposite side of the shadow to the right side.	Evidence—1
We could make a shadow because the light is in a straight line until it's blocked.	Reasoning—1
Student B	
When we move the light source one way, the shadow moves the opposite.	Claim—1
We shined the flashlight to the right and the shadow went to the left. When we shine the light to the left, the shadow goes to the right.	Evidence—2
Light always travels in a straight line because when we shone the laser through the Jell-O™, it went in a straight line.	Reasoning—1
Student C	
When we move the light source one way, the shadow goes the other way. The shadow is in a straight line opposite the light source.	Claim—2
When we put the light source to the right, the shadow moved to the left. When we moved the light source to the left, the shadow moved to the right. When we held it straight ahead, the shadow went behind the pipe cleaner person.	Evidence—3
Light travels in a straight ray until it is blocked. We made a shadow with a pipe cleaner person and it blocked the light source to make a shadow.	Reasoning—2
Student D	
The shadow is made opposite the object by the angle of the light source.	Claim—1
The evidence is that when you shine the light source in a different direction, the shadow of the objects is the opposite direction of the light source.	Evidence—1
The reasoning is that the light travels in a straight line until the pipe cleaner person blocks it to make a shadow.	Reasoning—2

Discuss Providing Students with Feedback (Time: 15 minutes)

Ask the participants what types of feedback or strategies they would use to support these four students in writing stronger scientific explanations. Ask if there are other strategies they use with their own students. Discuss and/or post the following key points:

- What to comment on:
  - Inclusion and quality of the claim, evidence, reasoning, and potential rebuttal
  - Accuracy and thoroughness of the science content

- Holistic quality of the scientific explanation
- How to comment:
  - Give explicit and clear feedback.
  - Point out strengths and weaknesses.
  - Provide suggestions on how to improve.
  - Ask questions to promote deeper thinking.

Design Specific Rubric and Analyze Student Work (Time: 30 minutes)

Tell participants that they will now be working in small groups to design a specific rubric for the assessment task that they designed during Session 7. The group should begin by writing an ideal student response and then analyzing that response to determine the number of components and the complexity of the components. The participants may also want to look at the samples of student writing to inform their rubric. Then the group should adapt the base rubric to develop a specific rubric for the assessment task.

After designing the rubric, the participants should use it to score some of the student responses. They should pick three to four student responses, and each group member should score the work individually. Then the group members should share and discuss their scores. They should use this discussion to inform any revision of the rubric as well as to discuss potential student feedback that they could provide these students.

Ask participants to reconvene as a whole group and discuss different lessons learned. Discuss and/or post the following questions:

- How was this process similar to and different from how you have designed and used rubrics in the past?
- What information did the rubrics provide you about student learning?
- What challenges arose as you were designing the rubric?
- What remaining questions do you have?

Extension

- If participants are focusing on younger students, you may want to discuss examples of student writing through a more informal process that does not include a rubric.
- Distribute copies of Handout 15—Student Examples—What Happens When You Mix Solids? Explain that participants are going to look at four writing examples from first-graders to determine what a teacher might think about when assessing student writing. The examples are from the lesson *What Happens When You Mix Solids?* This lesson is part of a larger unit on states of matter. Be sure to explain that these first-graders are just beginning to write explanations on their own.
- Have the participants think about the following questions as they look at the sample first-grade explanations:
  - How would you assess each student's understanding of the concept?
  - What are the strengths and weaknesses in the students' claims and evidence?
  - What struggles are the students having with writing their evidence? (Young students often do not include specifics in their evidence. In this case, the students could have included some specifics about the materials they tested such as the rice stayed white and it still had the same shape.)

> o   What would you say is an ideal claim and evidence for this lesson? (Claim: The solids could be separated after mixing them. They still had the same color and shape. Evidence: The rice was still white and had a rice shape. The sand was still tan and was in little pieces. We could pick out the rice.)
>
> o   As a teacher looking at the students' work, what would you choose to work on as part of your next lesson to guide students in the process of writing scientific explanations?

Homework

- Ask participants to read Chapter 7.

- Remind participants to video record their teaching during a part of the instructional sequence in which the class is engaged in discussion and using the scientific explanation framework. They should then watch the video and select a two- to three-minute video clip to share at the final session. The video clip will be examined to reflect on the role of the framework in discussions, the interactions between the students, and the role of the teacher in supporting classroom discussions.

SESSION 9

Supporting Learning over Time

Learning Goals

1. To consider how the CER framework can be used to create a classroom culture that gives priority to evidence and explanation

2. To share and reflect on a video of participants' own practices associated with engaging students' in constructing explanations in science

3. To reflect on teachers' development across the period of the book study

4. To identify potential next steps for using the scientific explanation framework to support learning over time

Materials

- Chart paper and markers
- Video 7.1—Shaping a Science Community
- Computer (with speakers) and LCD projector

Session Plan

Discuss Norms of Participation in Science Learning (Time: 15 minutes)

Discuss with the participants the idea that science is a way of knowing that includes specific ways of writing, talking, doing, thinking, and reasoning. Creating a classroom culture around the scientific explanation framework supports students not only in their science writing but also in their scientific reasoning and science talk. This session will focus on how to use the framework to develop a classroom community that prioritizes the construction of scientific explanations using evidence.

Introduce three features that can support the creation of a classroom culture that prioritizes scientific explanation. *Discuss and post the following three features on a piece of chart paper or display them using an LCD projector:*

1. The role of the scientific explanation framework in the discussion
    - The language of claim, evidence, and reasoning should be used by both teacher and students.

2. Active listening and patterns of talk
   - The language of agree/disagree requires students to listen to one another and weigh the thinking of their peers against their own ideas.
   - Over time the classroom community works together to negotiate meaning.
3. A culture of constructive criticism
   - Creating a classroom culture in which students agree and disagree with one another requires a safe and trusting environment.
   - Encourage students to establish the ground rules for how they want their science talks to be.
   - Prompt students to use talk moves until they can do so with fluency.
   - Remind students that disagreements are about aspects of the CER framework, not personal issues.

Discuss with participants how each of these three features can support classroom discussion in which students justify their ideas and build off the ideas of their peers.

Watch and Discuss Video of Ms. Hershberger's Classroom (Time: 15 minutes)

Show Video 7.1 from Ms. Hershberger's classroom in which students discuss how they want their science class to be. As participants watch the video, ask them to consider how the three features are incorporated into this discussion. After watching the video, discuss each of the features. Emphasize that the features exhibited are (1) using the scientific explanation framework, (2) engaging in active listening and considering the ideas of others, and (3) supporting a culture of constructive criticism.

Share and Discuss Science Teaching Videos (Time: 30 minutes)

Have teachers meet in small groups from the Session 6 instructional sequence planning session. Each teacher should share with his or her group the two- to three-minute clip of the group's instructional sequence and teaching strategy. The group should reflect on the video clip, keeping in mind the components of the instructional sequence. *Post the following directions and discussion questions on a piece of chart paper or display them using an LCD projector to support the group work:*

1. Have each teacher share his or her video clip. The teacher should share why he or she selected the particular clip and what he or she wants to receive feedback on.
2. The small group discusses each video clip and provides feedback to the teacher:
   - What component of the instructional sequence is shown in the clip?
   - What was the role of the scientific explanation framework?
   - What was the pattern of teacher and student talk?
   - What types of questions did the teacher ask?
   - What were some strengths of the video clip?
   - What are some suggestions for improvement if the lesson is taught again?

After the groups share and discuss their video clips, reconvene as a whole group. Discuss and/or post the following questions:

- What were some patterns people observed in terms of the role of the framework? Patterns of teacher and student talk? Types of questions used by the teachers?

- What did you learn from your discussion with your colleagues?

- What remaining questions do you have?

Reflect on Your Journey (Time: 30 minutes)

Acknowledge to participants that teaching science in this way can be challenging even for the most experienced teachers. Have teachers get into small groups and discuss the following questions about their experiences with learning to teach science with an emphasis on engaging students in scientific explanation. Ask each group to select a recorder to write main points from the small-group discussions on chart paper to post around the classroom. *During the discussion post the following questions on a piece of chart paper or display them using an LCD projector:*

- What are some of the rewards of teaching science as explanation?

- What are some of the challenges in changing your practice to teach science in this way?

- What are some strategies you will use to support your ongoing development for teaching science as explanation?

If it makes sense to do so, you can share video clips from an example study group to get the discussion going. After the groups share and discuss their ideas, reconvene as a whole group. Discuss and/or post the following questions:

- What were some of the rewards and challenges that you discussed?

- What strategies will you attempt to support your continued development?

- What did you learn from the discussion with your colleagues?

- What remaining questions do you have?

Thank teachers for their participation in the study group. Offer to provide follow-up support if appropriate.

Homework

- Ask participants to read Chapter 7.

- Have participants develop a written plan of how they will incorporate the scientific explanation framework into their classrooms in the future. What lessons did they learn from Book Study? What questions do they have that they hope to continue to investigate in their classrooms in the future?

HANDOUT PAGES

HANDOUT 1—AIR BAG INVESTIGATION

Question: How strong is a bag of [compressed] air?

Purpose

In this investigation you will make predictions and observations about a plastic bag filled with air.

Predictions

What do you think you will and won't be able to lift with your bag of [compressed] air?

Items It Will Lift	Items It Won't Lift

Data Collection

Record your observations in the following table.

Item	Observations	Item	Observations

Conclusion

Write a **scientific explanation** that answers the question and uses evidence to support your answer. Include scientific principles about the properties of air in your explanation.

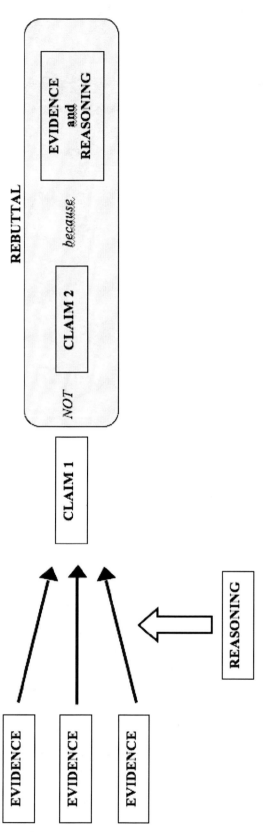

Student A

How Strong is a Bag of Air?

1. Predict some items that you think your bag of air will lift and some that it won't lift?

Will lift?	Results	Won't lift?	Results
glue stick	yes	laptop	yes
1 paper	yes	book bag	yes
paperclip	yes	box of blocks	yes
pencil	yes	Person	yes

2. Record your air bag investigation data by writing yes or no in the results column of the data chart and drawing a picture.

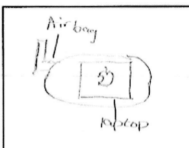

3. Write a scientific explanation:

Claim: A bag of air is very strong.

Evidence: My evidence is if lifted a laptop, a person, and a bookbag.

Reasoning: A bag of air is very strong because I thought it could not lift something heavy but, it did.

Student B

How Strong is a Bag of Air?

1. Predict some items that you think your bag of air will lift and some that it won't lift?

Will lift?	Results	Won't lift?	Results
Water bottle	Yes	A person	Yes
Book	Yes	a clock	Yes
Rubber band	Yes	a Dictionary	Yes
Feather	Yes	Brick	Yes

2. Record your air bag investigation data by writing yes or no in the results column of the data chart and drawing a picture.

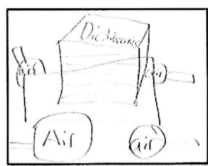

3. Write a scientific explanation:

Claim: A bag of air is very strong because it lifted heavy objects.

Evidence: The air bag lifted 10 dictionaries, 3 people, a ladder, and a brick. I was able to lift everything I predicted it wouldn't.

Reasoning: Air has weight because it lifted heavy objects and it takes weight to lift things. Air takes up space because when we blowed air in the bag we could see that the bag was full.

Student C

How Strong is a Bag of Air?

1. Predict some items that you think your bag of air will lift and some that it won't lift?

Will lift?	Results	Won't lift?	Results
feather	Yes	globe	Yes
eraser	Yes	boombox	Yes
foamstick	Yes	guitar	Yes
crayon	Yes	teacher chair	Yes

2. Record your air bag investigation data by writing yes or no in the results column of the data chart and drawing a picture.

3. Write a scientific explanation:

Claim: I think air is stronger than anything in the world because the airbag lifted heavy things.

Evidence: It lifted a teacher chair and the guitar. I even lifted three people when we worked together using our airbags and a board.

Reasoning: Air is so strong because it lifted up everything I didn't think it would.

Student D

How Strong is a Bag of Air?

1. Predict some items that you think your bag of air will lift and some that it won't lift?

Will lift?	Results	Won't lift?	Results
tissuebox	yes	people	yes
marker	yes	dictionaries	yes
jacket	yes	chair	yes
ham sandwich	yes	laptop	yes

2. Record your air bag investigation data by writing yes or no in the results column of the data chart and drawing a picture.

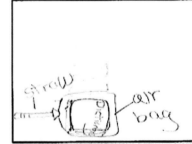

3. Write a scientific explanation:

Claim: A bag of air is very strong, because it lifted things I didn't think it would lift.

Evidence: We lifted 3 people, 10 dictionaries, a chair, and laptop with the bag of air.

Reasoning: Air is strong and it takes up space. The air filled the space of the bag.

HANDOUT 4—VARIATIONS OF THE SCIENTIFIC EXPLANATION FRAMEWORK

Level of Complexity	Framework Sequence	Description of Framework for Students
Simple ↓ **Complex**	**Variation #1** 1. Claim 2. Evidence	**Claim** • A statement that answers the question **Evidence** • Scientific data that support the claim
	Variation #2 1. Claim 2. Evidence • Multiple pieces	**Claim** • A statement that answers the question **Evidence** • Scientific data that support the claim • Includes multiple pieces of data
	Variation #3 1. Claim 2. Evidence • Multiple pieces 3. Reasoning	**Claim** • A statement that answers the question **Evidence** • Scientific data that support the claim • Includes multiple pieces of data **Reasoning** • A justification for why the evidence supports the claim using scientific principles
	Variation #4 1. Claim 2. Evidence • Multiple pieces 3. Reasoning 4. Rebuttal	**Claim** • A statement that answers the question **Evidence** • Scientific data that support the claim • Includes multiple pieces of data **Reasoning** • A justification for why the evidence supports the claim using scientific principles **Rebuttal** • Describes alternative explanations, and provides counterevidence and reasoning for why the alternative explanation is not appropriate

Steps 1 and 2: Specify the Learning Goal and Design Complexity of the Learning Task

Where in the curriculum will you include the CER learning task?

Identify opportunities for students to engage with phenomena and collect data.

Identify scientific principles that students will use to show why data count as evidence for a claim.

Aspects of Steps 1 and 2	Your Plan
Specify your learning goal. • What do you want students to be able to "do" with the science knowledge? • Develop a *learning performance* that combines science content and scientific inquiry practice. Be sure it reflects the goal of having students construct an explanation from evidence.	
Design the complexity of the learning task. • Consider the openness of the question. • Attend to the complexity of the type and amount of data	
Vary the complexity of the CER framework (Handout 4). For example, Variation #2 (claim and multiple pieces of evidence).	

Step 3: Use the Planning Matrix

Question	Claim	Evidence	Reasoning	Activity
Questions should be testable in some way. Students should know what the question is that they are trying to answer through their investigations.	A claim is a statement based on evidence that answers the question. *These statements should reflect unit science concepts and/or student learning outcomes.*	Evidence is a pattern in observations/data from which the claim is generated.	Reasoning is a justification that uses scientific principles to further explain the claim and evidence.	Activities should be carefully selected to provide the appropriate opportunities for observations/data collection necessary for evidence.

Craft an ideal and complete written scientific explanation from a student perspective. Include the question, claim, evidence, and reasoning.

Step 4: Examine the Learning Task for Coherence

Aspects of a Coherent Content Storyline	Your Justification
Does the learning task reflect one main science idea that is consistent with the learning goal?	
Is there a focus question and does it align with the learning goal?	
Are student activities, especially those that involve data collection, related to the main science idea?	
If there is more than one student activity, are they sequenced appropriately?	
If you are using other representations, such as analogies, diagrams, and models, are they matched to the main science idea?	
How will you synthesize the key ideas of the lesson?	
How can the science ideas from this learning task be linked to other content ideas in the unit?	

HANDOUT 6—BATTERY AND BULB LESSON TRANSCRIPT

Video 4.1–Talk Moves

Teacher: Who thinks that this one is not gonna work? Not gonna work? Adam, what are you thinking about number 3?

Adam: Number 3?

Teacher: Yeah.

Adam: I think that it will not work, because the tip of the light bulb is not even touching the battery.

Teacher: Alright, let's look at number 4, Tynan. Talk to us about number 4. What do you think about number 4, Tynan?

Tynan: I'm not sure but I said yes because it . . . the wire's still touching one of the metal parts. It's sort of like number 1, except both, except the wire is touching the same metal side that the light bulb is on.

Teacher: So, do people agree or disagree with Tynan? Eleanor?

Eleanor: I disagree because the negative part of the battery is not touching the bulb.

Teacher: So, what do you think, Becky?

Becky: I think it will not work, because I think it needs to be touching the negative and positive side.

Teacher: What do you think, Nate?

Nate: I agree with Tynan.

Teacher: You agree with Tynan? Go ahead.

Nate: Because it's still touching a power source and they're both still touching a power source. I really don't think it matters that they're both touching the same one or touching different ones.

Teacher: Kaylen, what are you thinking?

Kaylen: I agree, I think it will work—uh, won't work because there's not enough power if it's just on one side to light the light bulb.

Teacher: How do you know that?

Kaylen: Well, I predict that.

Teacher: Do you have any evidence, Maria Lan, about that?

Maria Lan: It's not going to light because, uh, you need the negative and positive end.

Teacher: How do you know that?

Eleanor: I know that because when we were trying to figure out how you could get the light bulb to light, if you try to just have it attached to one end it wouldn't work.

Teacher: What do you think about 1, Ameen? What do you think about number 4?

Ameen: I don't really think so because you need power from the other side of the battery to get into there, too, because there won't be that much energy to get inside of it.

Teacher: What do you think, Adam? About number 4, what are you thinking?

Adam: I'm thinking that it will work because even though the wire is on the same side of the light bulb I think it still would work.

Teacher: So we have some disagreement about this one. What do you think, Sam? I haven't heard from you. What do you think about number 4?

Sam: Yes.

Teacher: Will work? Why?

Sam: What I heard Tynan saying it kind of . . . it kind of made some sense.

Teacher: Why?

Sam: I think it's basically like this, like what we tested last time but it's just littler.

Teacher: What do you think, Owen?

Owen: I think it won't work because I think it will need to touch the negative and positive parts of the battery for it to light up.

Teacher: So we have Adam and Tynan and who else?

Student: Me.

Student: Me.

Teacher: Nate is thinking that it will work. And we have some definite people . . .

Nate: I think we should test it.

Teacher: Well, we're definitely going to. We're going to finish talking about the other ones, but we're definitely going to test it.

Handout 7—Writing Scaffold for Adaptation Investigation

Results

Beak	Marbles	Pennies	Popsicle® Sticks	Red Water
Chopsticks				
Spoon				
Tweezers				
Straw				

Conclusion:
[Write an argument that answers the question: Which bird beak is the best adaptation for this environment?]

Claim
[Write a sentence stating which bird's beak is the best adaptation for this environment.]

Evidence
[Provide scientific data to support your claim. The evidence should include the amount of food (marbles, pennies, popsicle® sticks, and red water) that the bird with the adapted beak ate.]

Reasoning
[Explain why your evidence supports your claim. Describe what an adaptation is and why your evidence allowed you to determine which bird beak was the best adaptation.]

Figure 4.2 from *What's Your Evidence?*

HANDOUT 8—INSTRUCTIONAL SEQUENCE FOR CONSTRUCTING SCIENTIFIC EXPLANATIONS

Sequence Component	Description	Comments
Assessing prior knowledge	Find out what students *think* they know about the big idea you will be investigating.	
Framing the question	Introduce students to the question that will drive the investigation.	
Making predictions	Get students to make a commitment about what they think will happen during the investigation. This can be another way of assessing prior knowledge.	
Collecting, recording, and interpreting data	Provide students with an opportunity to test their predictions, collect and record data/ observations, and represent and make sense of the data (e.g., create a graph, identify patterns).	
Constructing a scientific explanation	Use the evidence to create a statement that answers the question (i.e., claim). Integrate reasoning to further develop the relationship between claim and evidence.	

HANDOUT 9—INTEGRATE INSTRUCTIONAL SEQUENCE FOR CONSTRUCTING SCIENTIFIC EXPLANATIONS

Steps 1 and 2: Specify the Learning Goal and Design Complexity of the Learning Task

Aspects of Steps 1 and 2	Your Plan
Specify your learning goal. • What do you want students to be able to "do" with the science knowledge? • Develop a *learning performance* that combines science content and scientific inquiry practice. Be sure it reflects the goal of having students construct an explanation from evidence.	
Design the complexity of the learning task. • Consider the openness of the question. • Attend to the complexity of the type and amount of data	
Vary the complexity of the CER framework (Handout 4). For example, Variation #2 (claim and multiple pieces of evidence).	

Step 3: Use the Planning Matrix

Question	Claim	Evidence	Reasoning	Activity
Questions should be testable in some way. Students should know what the question is that they are trying to answer through their investigations.	A claim is a statement based on evidence that answers the question. *These statements should reflect unit science concepts and/or student learning outcomes.*	Evidence is a pattern in observations/data from which the claim is generated.	Reasoning is a justification that uses scientific principles to further explain the claim and evidence.	Activities should be carefully selected to provide the appropriate opportunities for observations/data collection necessary for evidence.

Craft an ideal and complete written scientific explanation from a student perspective. Include the question, claim, evidence, and reasoning

Step 4: Consider Coherence of Storyline

Aspects of a Coherent Content Storyline	Your Justification
Does the learning task reflect one main science idea that is consistent with the learning goal?	
Is there a focus question and does it align with the learning goal?	
Are student activities, especially those that involve data collection, related to the main science idea?	
If there is more than one student activity, are they sequenced appropriately?	
If you are using other representations, such as analogies, diagrams, and models, are they matched to the main science idea?	
How will you synthesize the key ideas of the lesson?	
How can the science ideas from this learning task be linked to other content ideas in the unit?	

Step 5: Integrate Instructional Sequence for Constructing Scientific Explanations

Sequence Component	Your Plan
Assessing prior knowledge	
Framing the question	
Making predictions	
Collecting, recording, and interpreting data	
Constructing a scientific explanation	

Which strategy do you plan to use to support the instructional sequence for scientific explanation: use a KLEW(S) chart, critique a sample explanation, or debate a peer scientific explanation? Describe your approach.

Assessment Topic: Force and Motion

Step 1: Identify and Unpack the Content Standard

Content standard

The greater the force is, the greater the change in motion will be. The more massive an object is, the less effect a given force will have (AAAS, 2009, 4F/E1bc).

Break down the content standard into different ideas and clarify.

- *A force is a push or a pull.*
- *A greater force is a larger push or a larger pull.*
- *A larger force will cause a greater change in the motion of an object such as making an object move faster, move slower, or change direction.*

Identify common student misconceptions

- *Students think force is a property of the object and is not influenced by the size of the push or the pull* (Driver et al., 1994).
- *Students think motion exists in only two categories—moving and not moving—rather than considering the speed of an object* (Driver et al., 1994).

Step 2: Select Scientific Explanation Level of Complexity

What *variation* of the framework do you want students to include in their response?

(For example, complexity of the evidence, inclusion and complexity of reasoning, and inclusion of rebuttal)

Variation #3
1. *Claim*
2. *Evidence*
   • *Multiple pieces*
3. *Reasoning*

Students are expected to support their claim with multiple pieces of evidence. Furthermore, they should include reasoning, although the reasoning is relatively simple and includes only one component.

Step 3: Create Learning Performance

Combine the science content with the variation of the framework.

Content Standard	Practice	Learning Performance
The greater the force is, the greater the change in motion will be. The more massive an object is, the less effect a given force will have (AAAS, 2009, 4F/E1bc).	Use data to construct a reasonable explanation (NRC, 1996, A: 1/4, K-4). Communicate investigations and explanations (NRC, 1996, A: 1/5, K-4).	*Students construct a scientific explanation stating a claim about the motion of an object, providing evidence in the form of data about the force applied to an object and the motion of the object (e.g., distance traveled, speed, or direction), and reasoning about the greater the force is, the greater the change in motion will be.*

Step 4: Write the Assessment Task

Students built vehicles that looked like the following:

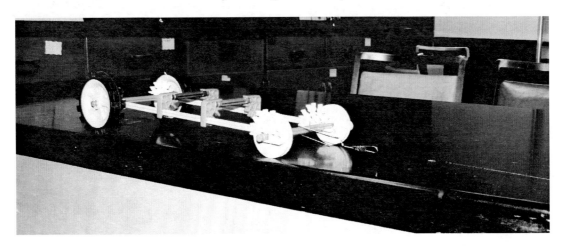

In this investigation, the string on the end of the car is attached to washers that hang off the table. The washers act as the force that causes the car to move. The students change the number of washers hanging off the table to investigate the relationship between the weight of the washers (i.e., the amount of force) and the speed of the vehicle. Specifically, Ms. Robinson asked them to test the vehicle using 2 washers, 4 washers, 8 washers, and 16 washers. After completing the investigation, she gave them the following writing prompt and reminded them to write a scientific explanation that included a claim, evidence, and reasoning:

Does the weight of the washers change the speed of the vehicle?

Assessment Topic: _____

Step 1: Identify and Unpack the Content Standard

Content standard

Break down the content standard into different ideas and clarify.

Identify common student misconceptions.

Step 2: Select Scientific Explanation Level of Complexity

What *variation* of the framework do you want students to include in their response?

(For example, complexity of the evidence, inclusion and complexity of reasoning, and inclusion of rebuttal)

Step 3: Create Learning Performance

Combine the science content with the variation of the framework.

Step 4: Write the Assessment Task

HANDOUT 12—BASE SCIENTIFIC EXPLANATION RUBRIC

LEVEL		Claim	Evidence	Reasoning	Rebuttal
		A statement or conclusion that answers the original question/problem.	*Scientific data that support the claim. The data need to be appropriate and sufficient to support the claim.*	*A justification that connects the evidence to the claim. It shows why the data count as evidence by using appropriate and sufficient scientific principles.*	*Recognizes and describes alternative explanations, and provides counterevidence and reasoning for why the alternative explanation is not appropriate.*
	0	Does not make a claim, or makes an inaccurate claim.	Does not provide evidence, or provides only inappropriate evidence (evidence that does not support the claim).	Does not provide reasoning, or provides only inappropriate reasoning.	Does not recognize that alternative explanation exists and does not provide a rebuttal, or makes an inaccurate rebuttal.
	Varies from 1 to 5	Makes an accurate but incomplete claim.	Provides appropriate, but insufficient evidence to support the claim. May include some inappropriate evidence.	Provides reasoning that connects the evidence to the claim. May include some scientific principles or justification for why the evidence supports the claim, but not sufficient.	Recognizes alternative explanations and provides appropriate but insufficient counterevidence and reasoning in making a rebuttal.
		Makes an accurate and complete claim.	Provides appropriate and sufficient evidence to support the claim.	Provides reasoning that connects the evidence to the claim. Includes appropriate and sufficient scientific principles to explain why the evidence supports the claim.	Recognizes alternative explanations and provides appropriate and sufficient counterevidence and reasoning when making rebuttals.

HANDOUT 13—SPECIFIC SCIENTIFIC EXPLANATION RUBRIC—
HOW DOES THE POSITION OF THE LIGHT SOURCE CHANGE THE POSITION OF THE SHADOW?

	Claim	Evidence	Reasoning
	A statement or conclusion that answers the original question/problem.	*Scientific data that support the claim. The data need to be appropriate and sufficient to support the claim.*	*A justification that connects the evidence to the claim. It shows why the data count as evidence by using appropriate and sufficient scientific principles.*
0	Does not make a claim, or makes an inaccurate claim like—"Light does not create shadows."	Does not provide evidence, or provides only inappropriate evidence or vague evidence like "the data show me it is true" or "our investigation is the evidence"	Does not provide reasoning, or provides only inappropriate reasoning like "light is not important for shadows."
1	Makes an accurate but incomplete claim that includes 1 of the following 2 pieces: • The shadow falls in a straight line from the light source. • The shadow moves in the opposite direction of the light source.	Provides 1 of the following 3 pieces of evidence: • When I held the flashlight on the left, the shadow was to the right. • When I held the flashlight behind the person, the shadow moved straight in front. • When I held the flashlight on the right, the shadow was to the left. OR Makes a general statement about how the shadow is opposite the direction of the light without specifying all of the 3 specific observations from the investigation. May also include inappropriate evidence.	Provides 1 of the following 2 reasoning components: • Light travels in a straight line. • Objects (like the pipe cleaner person) block light to create a shadow.
2	Makes an accurate and complete claim that includes 2 of the following 2 pieces: • The shadow falls in a straight line from the light source. • The shadow moves in the opposite direction of the light source.	Provides 2 of the following 3 pieces of evidence: • When I held the flashlight on the left, the shadow was to the right. • When I held the flashlight behind the person, the shadow moved straight in front. • When I held the flashlight on the right, the shadow was to the left. May also include inappropriate evidence.	Provides 2 of the following 2 reasoning components: • Light travels in a straight line. • Objects (like the pipe cleaner person) block light to create a shadow.
3		Provides 3 of the following 3 pieces of evidence: • When I held the flashlight on the left, the shadow was to the right. • When I held the flashlight behind the person, the shadow moved straight in front. • When I held the flashlight on the right, the shadow was to the left.	

Student A

How does the position of the light source change the position of the shadow?

Use the pipe cleaner person, your outside shadow recording data, and a flashlight to recreate the way the shadows changed at 9:00, 12:00 and 2:30.

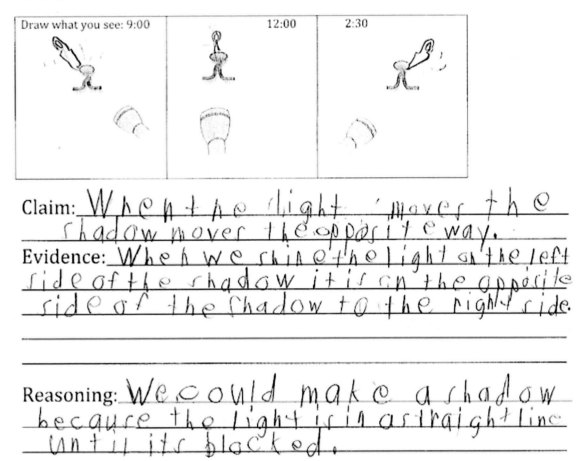

Claim: When the light movers the shadow mover the opposite way.

Evidence: When we shine the light on the left side of the shadow it is on the opposite side of the shadow to the right side.

Reasoning: We could make a shadow because the light is in a straight line until its blocked.

Student B

How does the position of the light source change the position of the shadow?

Use the pipe cleaner person, your outside shadow recording data, and a flashlight to recreate the way the shadows changed at 9:00, 12:00 and 2:30.

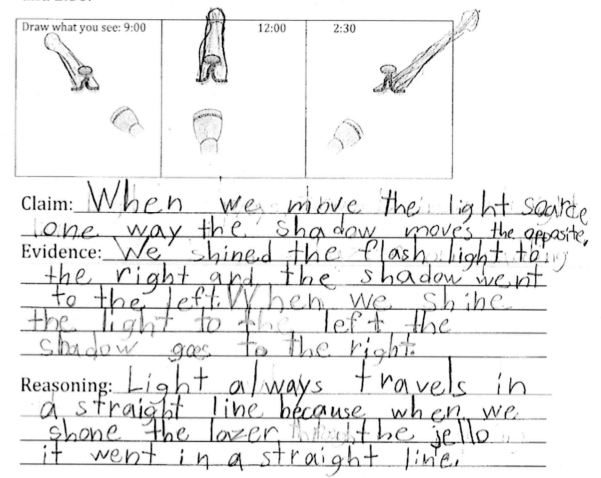

| Draw what you see: 9:00 | 12:00 | 2:30 |

Claim: When we move the light source one way the shadow moves the opposite.

Evidence: We shined the flashlight to the right and the shadow went to the left. When we shine the light to the left the shadow goes to the right.

Reasoning: Light always travels in a straight line because when we shone the lazer throught the jello it went in a straight line.

Student C

How does the position of the light source change the position of the shadow?

Use the pipe cleaner person, your outside shadow recording data, and a flashlight to recreate the way the shadows changed at 9:00, 12:00 and 2:30.

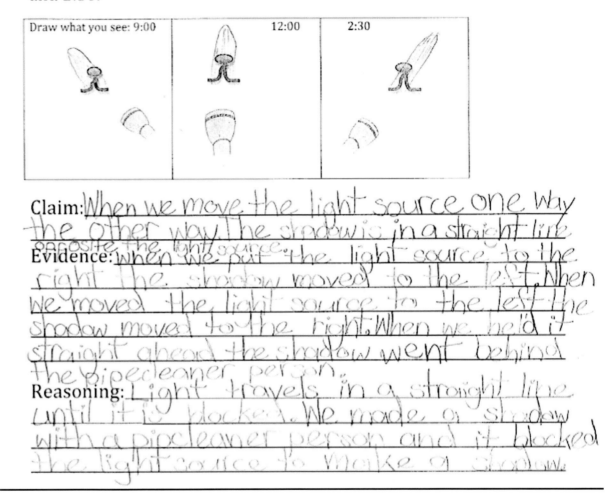

Claim: When we move the light source one way the other way the shadow is in a straight line opposite the light source.

Evidence: When we put the light source to the right the shadow moved to the left. When we moved the light source to the left the shadow moved to the right. When we held it straight ahead the shadow went behind the pipecleaner person.

Reasoning: Light travels in a straight line until it is blocked. We made a shadow with a pipecleaner person and it blocked the light source to make a shadow.

Student D

How does the position of the light source change the position of the shadow?

Use the pipe cleaner person, your outside shadow recording data, and a flashlight to recreate the way the shadows changed at 9:00, 12:00 and 2:30.

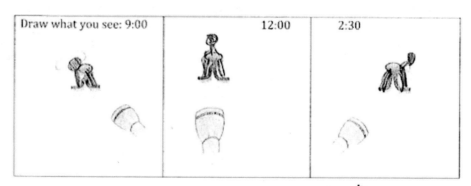

Claim: The shadow is made opposite the object by the angle of the light source.

Evidence: The evidence is that when you shine the light source in a different direction the shadow of the objects is the opposite direction of the light source.

Reasoning: The reasoning is that the light travels in a straight line untill the pipe cleaner person blocks it to make a shadow

Student A

What happens when you mix solids?

Mix the paper clips and the brass fasteners. What do you notice? Stir the mixture 10 times. Now what do you notice?

Diagram	Observation
	They don't chan'm shape or color

Can you separate the mixture? No

Mix the gravel and the blocks. What do you notice? Stir the mixture 10 times. Now what do you notice?

Diagram	Observation
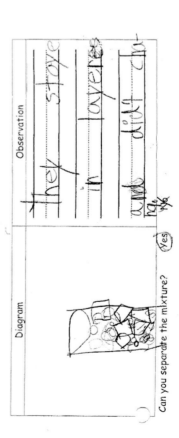	they stay in layers and did chu hd

Can you separate the mixture? Yes

Mix the rice and the sand. What do you notice? Stir the mixture 10 times. Now what do you notice?

Diagram	Observation
	We mixed but the sand stayed on the bottom. they didn' chang But

Can you separate the mixture? Yes

What happens when you mix solids? Write a claim. What is your evidence?

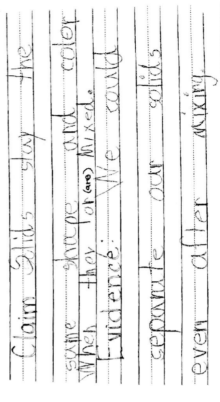

Claim: Solids stay the same shape and color when they (or are) mixed.

Evidence: We could separate our solids even after mixing.

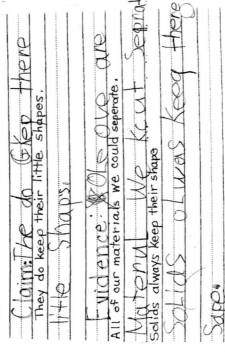

Student B

What happens when you mix solids?

Mix the paper clips and the brass fasteners. What do you notice? Stir the mixture 10 times. Now what do you notice?

Diagram	Observation
	They MiKs to They mixed together. deffm, But But you can see them. You can see them.

Can you separate the mixture?   (Yes)   No   theum,

Mix the gravel and the blocks. What do you notice? Stir the mixture 10 times. Now what do you notice?

Diagram	Observation
	They Kep They kept their shape. There safe

Can you separate the mixture?   (Yes)   No

Mix the rice and the sand. What do you notice? Stir the mixture 10 times. Now what do you notice?

Diagram	Observation
	The Rise Miks The rice mixes Is tgeth With together with sand. The Sand.

Can you separate the mixture?   (Yes)   No

What happens when you mix solids? Write a claim. What is your evidence?

Claim: The do Kep there They do keep their little shapes. lit le shapse

Evidence: Solie ove are All of our materials we could seperate. Material We Kept separat Solids always keep their shape. Solids always Keep there safe.

Student C

What happens when you mix solids?

Mix the paper clips and the brass fasteners. What do you notice? Stir the mixture 10 times. Now what do you notice?

Diagram	Observation
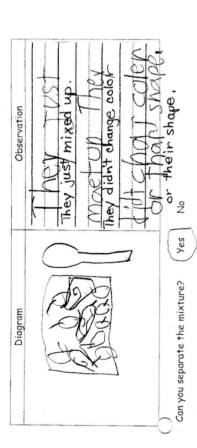	They just mixed up. Most of they They didn't change color it chang caler or their shape, or their shape.

Can you separate the mixture? Yes No

Mix the gravel and the blocks. What do you notice? Stir the mixture 10 times. Now what do you notice?

Diagram	Observation
	Wen we when we mixed them mix then they stay in layers, crystal layers,

Can you separate the mixture? Yes No

Mix the rice and the sand. What do you notice? Stir the mixture 10 times. Now what do you notice?

Diagram	Observation
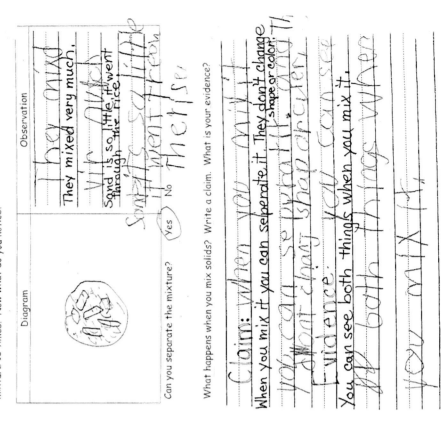	They mixed They mixed very much. Sand is so little, it went through the rice. something so little it went from the rise.

Can you separate the mixture? Yes No

What happens when you mix solids? Write a claim. What is your evidence?

Claim: When you mix When you mix it you can seperate it. They don't change shape or color. you can see preatty you can see preatly shap or color about chan shap or color. Evidence: you can see You can see both things when you mix it. My both things when you mix it.

Student D

What happens when you mix solids?

Mix the paper clips and the brass fasteners. What do you notice? Stir the mixture 10 times. Now what do you notice?

Diagram	Observation
	They mix up But don't change Shape or color

Can you separate the mixture?   Yes   No

Mix the gravel and the blocks. What do you notice? Stir the mixture 10 times. Now what do you notice?

Diagram	Observation
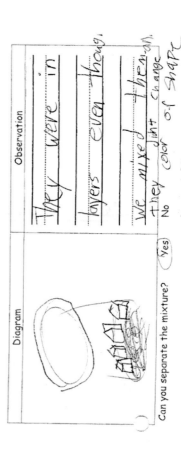	They were in layers even though. We mixed them. they didn't change color of shape

Can you separate the mixture?   Yes   No

Mix the rice and the sand. What do you notice? Stir the mixture 10 times. Now what do you notice?

Diagram	Observation
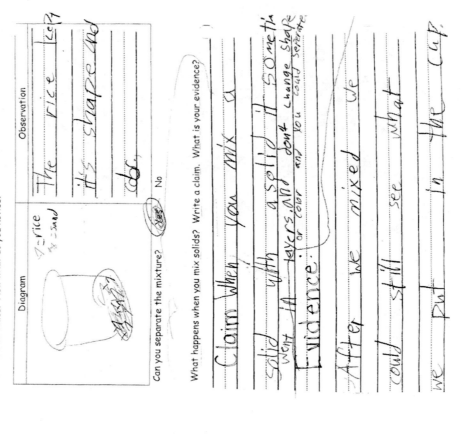	The rice keep it's shape and color.

Can you separate the mixture?   Yes   No

What happens when you mix solids? Write a claim. What is your evidence?

Claim When you mix a solid with a solid it sometime went in layers. And don't change shape or color and you could separate.

Evidence: After we mixed we could still see what we Put in the cup.